THE TOMBS OF A DEPARTED RACE

ILLUSTRATIONS OF IRELAND'S GREAT HUNGER

NIAMH O'SULLIVAN

CONTENTS

ARDCARA—CABIN OF J. DONOGHUE.

Figure 1 | "Ardcara—Cabin of J. Donoghue" (*PT*, February 7, 1846)

HORRIBLE SUFFERING, UTTER PENURY

From the mid-nineteenth century, it became possible to experience the wider world visually. The development of photography; the appearance of imagery in books, periodicals and pictorial newspapers; the growth in printmaking, greeting cards, posters and advertising; increased art production and greater opportunities for viewing art in the new museums, all brought imagery to the fore of popular culture, and into the flow of everyday life. Images not only helped to define relationships at a local or national level, but also brought diverse areas of the globe into contact with each other. The Great Irish Famine was one of the first global calamities to feature in popular illustration, as it was concurrent with the spread of new mass-market periodicals and the emergence of the phenomenon of humanitarian relief.

Popular visual representations of the Famine have served to heighten our responses to the catastrophe that devastated Ireland in the 1840s and early 1850s, however, the ubiquity in Irish history books of the familiar images of "Bridget O'Donnel and Children" [see **Figure 16** page 23] or "Woman Begging at Clonakilty," [see **Figure 31** page 41] for example, is testament to the use of illustrations as afterthoughts to the verbal accounts. Rarely examined in their own right, or subjected to critical visual analysis, early newspaper illustrations have been underestimated in their power to contribute meaningfully to our understanding of significant historical events. In the face of the destitution caused by the Famine, such illustrations may come across, by today's standards, as timid attempts to render the full horror of the events they depict, but by looking in more detail at how images worked in the new visual economies of the mid-nineteenth century, we can better grasp their impact on contemporaries and on subsequent generations.

A haunted past speaks of different things, casting its shadows down the generations. Maya Angelou said "there is no greater agony than bearing an untold story inside you," and that that story must be told "as one has known it, and lived it, and even died it" (vii). There are many ways of telling a story, and the appeal of the new pictorial journalism of the mid-nineteenth century lay in its claim to credibility and the capacity of the image to show the "truth." But visual representation is not an objective pursuit: measuring the extent to which images can tell the truth is fraught with difficulty, as every image contains components that implicitly or explicitly disclose the often contesting ideologies of the protagonists. It is by identifying these elements that we can go to the heart of what occurred, how it was reported and imaged, and subsequently interpreted. There is a philosophical difference between the attempts at truth telling in the new medium of illustration and the time-honored and deliberately politicized drawings of the cartoonist that puts satiric magazines beyond the scope of this essay. This pamphlet, therefore, examines the aesthetic, iconographic, technical and contextual roles of British newspaper illustration in telling the story of Ireland's Great Hunger.

Living conditions in Ireland **[Figure 1]** were the breeding ground for the Famine, the worst demographic catastrophe of nineteenth-century Europe.[1] The Great Hunger is best understood as a hundred-year event rather than a seven-year one—an outcome of systematic neglect by government. Over the decades of the eighteenth and early nineteenth centuries, Ireland staggered from one famine to the next, but the magnitude of the 1845–52 Famine was unparalleled.

The shocking conditions in which Irish people lived were long evident to eyewitnesses. As early as 1772, Benjamin Franklin observed:

a small part of the society are landlords, great noblemen, and gentlemen, extremely opulent, living in the highest affluence and magnificence. The bulk of the people are tenants, extremely poor, living in the most sordid wretchedness, in dirty hovels of mud and straw, and clothed only in rags. (98)

Dispossessed by settlers who expropriated their lands during the Conquest, Irish Catholic landowners and peasants had been driven to the bogs and mountainsides, most especially in the West, where they cultivated the potato. Even on such inhospitable soil, the potato grew abundantly. Potato cultivation on poor, rented plots, and occasional labor for low wages on larger farms, kept the Irish peasant in a state of perpetual subsistence, and on the verge of famine. More than one reporter described cabins **[Figure 2]** surrounded by middens, "the mud outside percolating to the interior, where it was trodden into a filthy adhesive glue by the feet and hoofs of the semi-naked children, pigs, fowl, and cattle" (*Times*, December 25, 1845). Newspaper accounts of rural life generally attributed the poverty of the Irish to an innate indolence and primitivism. Filth, hunger and despair were presented as *earned* conditions, in the face of the supposed patience, generosity and tolerance of their colonial masters. A "scientific" basis for such racialized prejudice was evident in illustrated examples of a distinct Irish "physiognomy."

Figure 2 | "Connemara Cabin" (*ILN*, August 12, 1843)

In the first half of the nineteenth century, the condition of the poor in Ireland was worse than in any other part of the British Isles. An appalled Gustave de Beaumont described how "[m]isery, naked and famishing ... follows you everywhere, and besieges you incessantly ... it importunes and terrifies you" (128). When *The Illustrated London News* was founded in 1842, a year not considered out of the ordinary for food shortages in Ireland, the paper carried a report (*ILN*, June 25, 1842) of another "calamitous season of starvation ... in the midst of apparent plenty." Poverty was exacerbated by a rapid growth in population. In 1750, the population of Ireland was approximately 2.6 million; in 1790, it had grown to just over 4 million; in 1846, it had more than doubled to 8.7 million. By 1845, 85 percent of the population lived on small plots of land, in extreme poverty. In his *Statistical Survey,* Isaac Weld described:

floors sunk in the ditches; the height scarcely enough for a man to stand upright; ... a few pieces of grass sods the only covering; and these extending only partially over the thing called a roof; the elderly people miserably clothed; the children all but naked. (477)

A *Pictorial Times* (*PT*) reporter visited a home scarcely exceeding the length of its occupier who had a wife and three children, concluding "[h]e will have almost as much space when laid in his grave" (February 7, 1846). A couple of weeks earlier, the paper had described an eight-feet-square cabin as pitch dark, "[t]he thatch was rotting: the cesspool up to the threshold of the doorway ..." (*PT*, January 24, 1846). *The Illustrated London News* noted "a bed or a blanket is a rare luxury, and nearly in all, their pig and manure-heap constitute their only property" (*ILN*, January 10, 1846). By 1848, Irish paupers numbered 1,876,541 "showing an increase of no less than 405,408 persons—a number equaling the population of New York" (*ILN*, March 24, 1849).

The average Irish male ate 12 to 14 lbs. of potatoes a day, women and children only slightly less. Fueled by this monotonous but cheap source of food which grew in poor soil, a family could subsist for almost the whole year on the yield of a one-acre plot. Although the lumper potato on which peasants were increasingly reliant was less nutritious than other varieties, it produced high yields, but it was also less resistant to blight. Against this backdrop of poverty and subsistence, the potato blight struck in 1845, wiping out the food supply of the poor. Caused by the fungus, *Phytophthora infestans*, the blight spread initially from Mexico to the United States—the spores carried by wind, rain and insects—and on to Europe, but its effects in Ireland were worse than anywhere else, due to the dominant reliance of Irish peasants on the potato.

Episodes of famine were common, but tended to occur in single years, and most people could adapt and survive; however, when the blight struck for a second consecutive year, the consequences were immediately devastating. *Pictorial Times* carried an illustration showing a distraught family, huddled together as their diseased food supply for an entire year rotted at their feet **[Figure 3]**. Five more harvest failures were to follow—complete crop failures in 1846 and 1848, and extensive failures in the other years—and the destructive effects were cumulative. There are few newspaper images of the blight itself, and little comment on the attendant effects of disease and hunger on the human body. Newspapers filtered out or avoided reports that might cast a critical eye on British government handling of the catastrophe.

Figure 3 | "Destitution in Ireland—Failure of the Potato Crop" (*PT*, August 22, 1846)

By 1847, famine had caused societal collapse, as the *Southern Reporter* lamented:

We are overwhelmed with distress; we are crushed with taxation; we are scourged by famine; and visited by pestilence. Our jails are full; our poor houses choked; our public edifices turned into lazar houses; our cities mendicities; our streets morgues; our churchyards fields of carnage. Our ordinary trade is gone; our people are partially demoralised. Society itself is breaking up; selfishness seizes upon all; class repudiates class; the very ties of closest kindred are snapt asunder. Sire and son, landlord and occupier, town and country repudiate each other, ceasing to co-operate—Terror and hunger, disease and death afflict us ... horrible suffering, utter penury ... (May 1, 1847)

Irish nationalist, John Mitchel argued that Ireland produced enough "to feed and clothe not nine but eighteen millions of people," yet "a government ship sailing into any harbor with Indian corn was sure to meet half a dozen sailing out with Irish wheat and cattle" (112). But, argued the Duke of Cambridge with unintentional Swiftian resonances: "Irishmen could live upon anything and there was plenty of grass in the field even though the potato crop should fail." (qtd. in *The Nation,* January 24, 1846).

Although historians differ as to the export statistics and the mortality implications, large quantities of butter, corn, peas, rabbits, salmon, oysters, herring, honey and seed, as well as porter and whiskey were exported. Ireland's contribution "to the power, and greatness, and riches of the most powerful empire of the earth" (*PT,* January 24, 1846) was conceded, yet economic ideology required that exports continued while the people who produced the food starved. In 1847, Lord Clarendon, Lord Lieutenant of Ireland, told the Prime Minister: "We shall equally be blamed for keeping them alive or letting them die, and we have only to select between the censure of the Economists or the Philanthropists." He went on to ask: "Which do you prefer?" (August 10, 1847. Letter book 1). Mitchel was in no doubt: *laissez faire* allowed for no political interference, provoking his observation that Ireland "died of political economy" (139). The logic of free trade had reduced the Irish to seeking pity rather than justice (Gibbons 2014).

The Rev. Dr. McEvoy, parish priest of Kells, described "vessels laden with our sole hopes of existence ... hourly wafted from our every port ... to feed the foreigner, leaving starvation and death the sure and certain fate of the toil and sweat that raised this food" (*The Nation*, October 25, 1845). The consequences of such disregard for life were not hard to foresee:

Will not a starving population become justly indignant when whole fleets, laden with the produce of our soil, are unfurling their sails and steering from our harbour, while the cry of hunger is singing in their ears? .... a wise government should at once issue an order prohibiting the exportation of provisions from this country, until the wants of the people have been sufficiently provided for? (*Waterford Freeman*, October 3, 1846)

Significantly, there are no images of food exportation in the British press, but there are many of British relief measures, and of Irish violence. In "Irish Armed Peasants Waiting for the Approach of a Meal Cart" (*PT*, October 30, 1847) **[Figure 4]**, three brigands lie in wait to attack a cart bringing relief to the poor. The aggression of the Irish is emphasized; the injurious consequences of placing food provisions under police protection is ignored. The accompanying illustration, "Meal Cart, Under Military Escort, Proceeding to a Relief Station, Clonmel" (*PT*, October 30, 1847) **[Figure 5]** is a tighter and more controlled image, showing a body of light dragoons effecting the transport of relief food. In each, the execution is adapted to inflect the narrative. In the former, the armed peasants dominate the landscape, in the latter, the serried forces of authority are integrated into their surroundings, suggesting a "benign" level of control. In the text separating the two, the contrast is drawn between "a wise and humane Government" doing their utmost for "a destitute and famine-stricken population" and the "lawless ruffians, who prefer the wages of crime to the fruits of honest industry ... [and] who rather spill human blood to purchase a meal, than till the generous earth for the sake of its abundance." (*PT*, October 30, 1847)

THE PICTORIAL TIMES. 281

IRISH ARMED PEASANTS WAITING FOR THE APPROACH OF A MEAL CART.

English; and we venture to anticipate that it will act upon the feelings of many of our expatriated countrymen much in the same manner as the song of the "Ranz des Vatches" is said to affect the Swiss exile. But however agreeable it may be to be sometimes reminded of home, we consider it very absurd to erect edifices of a purely English character in the peculiar climate of China. As it is, however, we find no very great fault with the general arrangements of the building, though some of the details are faulty enough; the windows especially being badly placed, and not very elegant in form. We may also usefully observe that architects might turn their attention to the subject of construction, as best adapted to the requirements of our various colonies, so differently situated as regards climate, people, and former religious observances, all of which should be considered to produce any new building that will harmonise with popular feelings, or the general appearance of the particular scenes in which they are placed.

FAMINE IN IRELAND.

The contrast of the two plates in this page suggests reflections anything but complimentary to Irish gratitude. On the one hand, we behold the operation of the arrangements of a wise and humane Government for supplying a destitute and famine-stricken population with the means of existence. The wheels of the meal cart creak under the burden which is to relieve hundreds of human beings

MEAL CART, UNDER MILITARY ESCORT, PROCEEDING TO A RELIEF STATION, CLONMEL.

Figure 4 | **"Irish Armed Peasants Waiting for the Approach of a Meal Cart"** (*PT*, October 30, 1847 [top]

Figure 5 | **"Meal Cart, Under Military Escort, Proceeding to a Relief Station, Clonmel"** (*PT*, October 30, 1847)

CRAWLING SKELETONS

The artists and illustrators of pictorial newspapers were classically trained in academies where the emphasis was on the human figure, learned from Greek and Roman casts.[2] Consequently, they had little or no experience of looking at unfiltered images of trauma, distress, or even poverty. When they became pictorial journalists, they had to abandon learned conventions and find new ways of visualizing what had not been imaginable before. Victorian audiences, accustomed to the idealized forms of history painting, found even the diluted images of Irish Famine distress in the illustrated press as shocking as we find famine reportage today.

Famine—in so far as it is the product of political negligence in a time of plenty, and often leaving little trace of intentionality—is an atrocity as violent and reprehensible as warfare. Atrocity embraces a wide range of competing definitions, and the iconography of atrocity is thus complicated by both aesthetic and ethical considerations. The art historical precedents—depictions of Greek and Roman wars, mythological slayings, religious extirpations, plagues and battles for Empire, were made at a remove in time and place from their audiences. Such art was intended to glorify, exhort or commemorate contemporary ideas, not to provide documentary accounts of the events they depict. Art representing terrible events, and intended for consumption by those contemporaneous with and adjacent to those events, is largely unprecedented before the Great Famine. A number of notable exceptions exist, significantly in the print medium: Jacques Callot's *Les Grandes Misères et Malheurs de la Guerre* (1633) **[Figure 6]** depicted acts committed by French troops against the civilians of Lorraine during the Thirty Years War. Showing massacre, rape, and torture, the series challenged conventional readings of heroism and victimization—the revenge of the peasants is just as violently portrayed as the pillaging by soldiers—raising problematic moral questions.

Figure 6 | Jacques Callot *The Plundering*, no. 4 from *Les Grandes Misères et Malheurs de la Guerre*

However, history painting insisted that important ideas required an appropriate size and scale. Callot's realism was accepted because, in a sense, it was executed in a nonthreatening medium—print—which, in turn, facilitated technical innovation. The genealogy of iconography usually passed through the painting line. Thus, when Benjamin West's *Death of General Wolfe* (1770) (National Gallery of Canada) was exhibited, it created shock waves through the Academy. By evoking the lamentation of Christ, West elevated Wolfe's dedication to the cause of the British in North America to a messianic level, but by depicting a near-contemporary event, he flaunted the conventions of history painting, creating a modern spectacle. When urged to paint the figures wearing togas, West replied: "the same truth that guides the pen of the historian should govern the pencil of the artist" (Galt 48).

The difficulty in finding an appropriate visual form for death is evident throughout the history of art. Rich and poor were equally awed by its inevitability. The dread of hell seemed more grounded in reality than the promise of heaven, hence more images exist of the fires of hell than the bliss of heaven. But images of death—being beyond the experience of the living—tended towards exaggeration and melodrama, until Realism hove into view.

The turn of the nineteenth century produced three works depicting death with a new and shocking immediacy: Jacques-Louis David's iconic French Revolution painting, the *Death of Marat* (1793) (Musées Royaux des Beaux-Arts, Brussels) became

Figure 7 | Théodore Géricault, *The Raft of Medusa*

perhaps the first convincingly earthly image of death; Antoine-Jean Gros' *Napoleon Bonaparte Visiting the Plague-Stricken in Jaffa* (1804) (Musée du Louvre), showed Napoleon touching one of the bubonic plague victims—as Christ did a leper—and was considered horrifying (although reassuringly "othered" by its Syrian setting); and then, in 1816, a French ship headed for a French colony in Africa ran aground (only fifteen survived, some reputedly having resorted to cannibalism), providing the inspiration for Théodore Géricault's *The Raft of Medusa* (1818–19) (Musée du Louvre) **[Figure 7]**. Géricault visited a morgue to ensure that his painting accurately portrayed death. But even as this new Realism in art was making its presence felt, the credible depiction of death remained a difficulty for most artists.

Figure 8 | Louis Duveau, *Plague of Elliant*

Two French paintings executed at the height of the Famine demonstrate transitionality in the pictorial rendition of death. Louis Duveau's *Plague of Elliant* (1849) (Musée des Beaux-Arts, Quimper) **[Figure 8]** has been ascribed Druidical or Celtic origins, and in that sense may be allegorical of the Famine.[3] Whatever about the technical difficulties of painting a scene in which a mother brings to the cemetery the bodies of her nine children who were killed by plague (their father driven mad from grief), attempting to communicate the attendant emotions led Duveau to visual histrionics, as if to demonstrate that commenting on catastrophe through evoking an heroic past was no longer considered equal to the task. The ultimate disavowal of history painting came immediately afterward with Gustave Courbet's *Burial at Ornans* (1849–50) (Musée d'Orsay)—a painting marking the death of his own loved but historically insignificant great-uncle—thus marking an epochal shift, contributing to the demise of history painting.

Given the long pre-eminence of history painting, the extent to which printmaking broke the mold in the nineteenth century is remarkable. Rather than signaling a depersonalization of the artist, or the artist's alienation from the work of art, it infused new opportunities into the visual arts. Being both less expensive and more accessible than painting, prints expanded the reach of artistic vision. And if the more successful visualizations of not only death but atrocity were in print form the most acute of Courbet's fellow innovators was Francisco Goya (1746–1828).

Figure 9 | Francisco Goya, *No hay quien los socorra (There is no one to help them)*

When Napoleon invaded Spain in 1808, the mass executions of Spanish citizens led to Goya's *Second of May 1808* and *Third of May 1808* (Museo del Prado), which he expanded in his Peninsular War series, *Los Desastres de la Guerra / Disasters of War* (1810–20). Here, Goya depicted murder, mutilation, torture and rape—demonstrating man's great inhumanity. But the second part of the series focused on the famine that ravaged Madrid between 1811 and 1812. *No hay quien los socorra (There is no one to help them)* (1863) **[Figure 9]**, for example, is an uncompromising work in which the shrouded bodies point unequivocally to death. People beg, they die, and are carried away for burial, highlighting Goya's role as witness, reporter and artist. In the seventeen famine plates (48–64), Goya created a new visual rhetoric in which he led the march towards modernity in art. In many, elements of the narrative are implicit rather than explicit, emphasizing the notion of visual intolerability. The prints straddle an apparent irreconcilability: realistic depictions of violence, created artistically. Robert Hughes believes that Goya's etchings are "more piercing in their documentary power, more savagely beautiful, and, in every way, more humanly moving ... they are the true ancestors of all great visual war reporting" (265).

Susan Sontag argues (18) that images can provide the frame for memories of events before they have occurred. In this sense, Goya adumbrated photography from the American Civil War, or photographs of lynching of black slaves, for example. Nevertheless, to suggest that Goya's *Los Desastres* are a form of photojournalism displaces the important art-historical traditions within which he operated. To some extent, *Los Desastres* are, or should have been, the iconographic antecedents of Irish Famine imagery. The fact that Goya's etchings were not published until 1863 may have denied Famine artists a model of representation they so badly needed, as they powerfully prefigure events in Ireland between 1845 and 1852. Life, it would seem, in certain extreme situations does sometimes imitate art.

"It is not so much by the [artist's] eye but *in* that of the beholder that the experience is decisively shaped," Max Kozloff argues (289). When atrocities are committed, and witnessed, responsibility passes to the observer—what Sontag calls, "co-spectatorship" (60). If Goya's caption, "I saw it," implicates the artist, *seeing* the artwork implicates the viewer. It is hard for us to understand the resistance of the authorities towards alleviating Famine distress in Ireland, but equally incomprehensible was the passivity of those who read of it, and saw the imagery of it. It is as shameful to look and do nothing as it is to look away. Sontag suggests that such images are invitational, asking us "to pay attention, to reflect, to learn, to examine the rationalizations for mass suffering offered by established powers" (91). In discussing a relational ethics of representation, Luke Gibbons argues that we should consider the spectator when presenting the point of view of the victim.

> *It is this two-way process in the dynamics of vision that is of central importance, for it implies that so far from negating experience, a certain reticence or refusal 'to show all' is required if an image is to elicit an ethical rather than a sensational, or even a sentimental response.* (13)

He goes on to argue for an "ethical aspect of the representations of atrocity, that is, the *obligation to look* rather than avert the gaze" (23). Undoubtedly, pictorial newspapers created such opportunities on a hitherto unprecedented scale.

HALF-CLAD SPECTRES

"Attack on a Potatoe Store" (*ILN*, June 25, 1842) **[Figure 10]**—the very first newspaper illustration of Ireland—appeared within a couple of weeks of the establishment of *The Illustrated London News* and, as an illustration, was unique aesthetically and politically. In coupling hunger and violence, it implicated the Irish in their own degraded condition. It is also the only illustration from this period to draw on the repertoire of fine art to convey the poverty of a people. The emphatic diagonal thrust, and the use of *repoussoir* figures to concentrate the action in the center, create a swirling vortex of violence that intensifies the narrative. The brute force of the protagonists and their thrall to Popery (note the Crucifix worn by the woman in the center) define from the outset the position of the newspaper vis-à-vis the Irish.

Figure 10 | "Attack on a Potatoe Store" (*ILN*, June 25, 1842)

It was over a year later before *The Illustrated London News* returned to the poor of Ireland in a carefully constructed spread of images called "Ireland and the Irish" (*ILN*, August 12, 1843). Here, in "Poor Children" **[Figure 11]** and "Idiot and Mother," **[Figure 12]** the elevated style of the previous illustration was played down, and a more prosaic style that conveys a less heroic, less dignified, less *entitled* portrayal of the Irish was adopted. This characterization was to continue, albeit with different inflections, into the twentieth century.

Figure 11 | "Poor Children" (*ILN*, August 12, 1843)

Prefigured by the satirical journal *Punch*, *The Illustrated London News*, founded in 1842, was the first pictorial newspaper to combine text and image. Less than a year later, *Pictorial Times* was established, and between them they spawned a host of others, on both sides of the Atlantic. Illustrated newspapers employed a huge stable of artists and correspondents, both in-house and around the world—their job to inform and entertain.[4]

Figure 12 | "Idiot and Mother" (*ILN*, August 12, 1843)

Comprising sixteen pages and featuring thirty-two engravings, the first weekly issue of *The Illustrated London News* sold an encouraging 26,000 copies **[Figure 13]**. Within weeks, it was selling 60,000 copies, and this rose to 100,000 by the peak of the Famine. It is speculated that for every purchaser there were on average thirty readers, so a significant proportion of the British public learned what they knew of the terrible events in Ireland from the illustrated press. And as these news engines had huge international reaches, so too did the rest of the world learn about the Great Hunger.

The relationship between image and text in the new illustrated weeklies shifted between issues, and from one artist to another. Coverage of Irish affairs swung from harrowing but sympathetic descriptions of poverty, disease and death, to condemnations of a savage and ignorant peasantry. More often, the correspondents were unsympathetic, and the artists were inclined to toe the line. But illustrations are open to different interpretations—even the most literal Famine images were viewed in accordance with the ideological interests of its readers.

Pictorial newspapers were read as avidly by the middle classes in Ireland as in England. By mid-century, literacy had been achieved by almost half the population in Ireland, though this was concentrated in the urban centers. The introduction of a national system of education in 1831 had generated a significant increase in readers. Even Erskine Nicol, whose paintings mercilessly mocked the Irish peasant, shows him in *A Knotty Point* (1853) (Ireland's Great Hunger Museum)[5] enjoying his good-for-nothing ways, with a newspaper in his hands. Ironically, newspapers gave little attention to this progress and continued to portray the Irish as homogenized and ignorant.

Illustration aesthetics derived from the pioneering work of Thomas Bewick who elevated wood engraving to a fine art. Initially, drawing and engraving were sequential stages, executed by the same hand. However, by the mid-nineteenth century, the separation of the stages—leading to a three-tiered system in which the artist, the illustrator/draftsman and the engraver were three different operators—became the norm. An understanding of the method of production is fundamental to understanding illustrations. The process was a protracted one, from the original sketch by the artist in the field, through the elaboration of the sketch by the home-based draftsman onto wood panels in the office, to the division of the image into blocks with several engravers working on each sketch, and the printing of the image. Given the complexities of the process, and the multiple personnel involved, not to mention the endless scope for editorial interference, there were multiple opportunities for cross-pollination or manipulation within each image.

Because a full-page illustration could take weeks to engrave, several engravers were put to work simultaneously on single images. Engravers (such as Joseph Swain, Ebenezer Landells, W. J. Linton and the Dalziel brothers) worked on close-grained wood, cut in transverse slices, about an inch thick, that were seasoned and racked in

Figure 13 | Illustration Composite

gradually heated rooms (ideally for five years). The blocks were then cut into three-and-a-half- by two-inch blocks, reassembled with brass nuts and bolts, and polished. The house illustrator/draftsman then drew on the block in reverse, and the lines were set across the joins, before dismantling. As fast as the draftsman finished a section, it was assigned in individual portions to the jobbing engravers, who never saw the whole of the drawing together. Thus, coherence and aesthetic considerations were sacrificed to the imperative of getting the paper out onto the street. Some illustrations, therefore, look better than others. In order to camouflage the fragmented nature of the process, the engravers tried to set the block breaks along the structural lines of an interior, or the trunk of a tree, for example, so that the architectonic or natural qualities of the image contributed to the conceptual effect.

The master engraver guided the tone and texture, while the jobbing engravers concentrated on the center sections. Each portion, therefore, had an edge prepared by the master engraver that smoothed the reunification of the final image.[6] This collaborative technique resulted in a house style that harmonized the various contributions. While we can search for identifying features in the work of individual artists, the analysis of their work is complicated by the fact that it is but one element in an aesthetic collective, so that is rarely possible to tell where one hand left off and another began.

Pictorial newspapers employed a relief method of print making, in which the white areas were cut away from the surface of a block, and the image then printed off the remaining inked surface. If a block was well engraved, there was virtually no limit to the number of impressions that could be taken. Images were quickly and relatively cheaply produced; and as the technique was type-high, for the first time, images could be printed on the same presses, and at the same time as type, to the point that the illustrations, as Brian Maidment puts it, "writhe about the page or else dominate and bully the surrounding text into compressed and unexpected columnular shapes" (2014). Almost half-a-million impressions—a typical number for a Christmas issue—if placed side-by-side (Mason Jackson, a later editor of *The Illustrated London News,* tells us), would extend over 660 miles in length. And as they were printed on both sides, this represented a printed surface extending over 1,115 miles (after deductions for margins), using almost eighty tons of paper and twenty-three hundredweight of printing ink, per week (266–67).

For a production to be successful, it needed to appeal to a mass audience, and be published fast, so that events did not overtake its currency. Thus illustrated newspapers employed "Specials," often distinguished artists such as John Gilbert, Randolph Caldecott or Gustave Doré. But if the technique tended to result in homogeneity, it would be a mistake to dismiss newspaper illustration as uniformly bland, as many of the better artists transcended the limitations of the medium. In many cases, the draftsman constructed the image from a written account in the office. But there is a qualitative difference between local and foreign illustration The draftsmen invested greater care in the sketches sent in by the Specials who worked abroad, as their own knowledge was less than that of the artist in the field.

But the difficult conditions under which Specials worked required the back-up skill of the home-based draftsmen to make the illustrations readable. As a result, their status was not much less than that of the Specials, giving rise to complications of authorship and acknowledgment. Sometimes the artists' notes were more detailed than the sketches. Sketches then had to be augmented and authenticated by maps and written accounts in other newspapers. Some newspapers even re-used vignettes where the same scene, figure or detail was appropriated for a new illustration, thereby disclosing the centrality of the home team to the end result.

To a considerable extent, editors cosseted readers from news that might unsettle them. Thus, representations of a massive social calamity such as the Famine were framed in such a way as to attract the target audience without overly disturbing it, in effect, drawing the reader into a complex relationship that kept their desire to know in check with their own self-interests, no less than the wider interests of Empire.

In sending their artists and correspondents to Ireland, the pictorial newspapers claimed to seek the "truth," but the real truth is that newspaper content is never simple or objective. Although some readers collected pictorial newspapers in bound folios over the year, for most readers one issue supplanted another, week by week.

Figure 14 | **"Ejectment of Irish Tenantry"** *(ILN, December 16, 1848)*

Neither the ethos of a periodical, nor the accuracy of an individual story, therefore, can be read from a single issue. The key to understanding Famine illustration then lies not in the individual images, but in their combination. And, examined serially, they emerge as an indictment of those who oversaw the catastrophe.

Figure 15 | **"An Eviction in the West of Ireland"** *(ILN*, March 19, 1881)

The bulk of the early Irish illustrations were straightforward portraits or scenic views. Gradually, the imagery took on a political hue: state trials, Repeal, the death of O'Connell, hunger, violence, insurrection, the visit of Queen Victoria to Ireland, etc. Increasingly, artists and editors had to negotiate dissonant views—those of the British government and public, and the Irish landlords and tenants. It follows that illustrations betimes clarify, expand, placate or contradict, not only each other but the text. And when it came to explaining the Famine, English newspapers often descended into righteous indignation and providentialist justification, unmasking a deep distaste for Irishness and poverty.

The success of illustrated newspapers lay in the purportedly symbiotic relationship between image and text. The written accounts often describe a barbaric race, usually visually countered by an increasingly enfeebled peasantry. Newspapers, however,

BRIDGET O'DONNEL AND CHILDREN.

Figure 16 | **"Bridget O'Donnel and Children"** (*ILN*, December 22, 1849)

are not transparent mirrors of the culture. Notwithstanding the assertions of their editors, they should not be seen as a direct 'reflection' of the attitudes of the time; rather, they were embroiled in the process of shaping those attitudes. W. J. T. Mitchell argues that instead of providing a transparent window on the world, images can present "a deceptive appearance of naturalness and transparency concealing an opaque, distorting, arbitrary mechanism of representation, a process of ideological mystification" (8). If the relationship between text and image is polysemous, oppositional positions within pictorial newspapers—between the visual and the verbal, and sometimes the pro and the anti—come down to the narrative complexity of the Famine, and the challenges in compressing cause and effect into a single image, beyond the reach of a simple "truth."

A further consideration is the state of evolution of the medium of wood engraving during the Famine period. Undoubtedly, illustrations of the Famine impress less than illustrations of the Land War produced later.[7] In "Ejectment of Irish Tenantry," (*ILN*, December 16, 1848) **[Figure 14]** an evicted family appeals to the Landlord's agent while the bailiffs tear down the roof and ruthlessly empty the family home. Notwithstanding Margaret Crawford's description of this as "one of the most exquisite engravings of the entire Famine collection" (83), the quality of the illustration is mixed. Although narratively rich, it has little of the visual coherence of the later "Eviction in the West of Ireland" (*ILN*, March 19, 1881) **[Figure 15]** by Aloysius O'Kelly, for example. The injustice in the case of the evicted Land League family is more clearly signaled, and this is achieved by greater artistic control (O'Sullivan, 2010, 37–38). The follow-up image to the former, "The Day after the Ejectment" (*ILN*, December 16, 1848) **[see Figure 38 page 48]**, showing the Famine family huddled in the ditch in the cold and rain, is less overwhelmed by detail, but the theatrical and posed stance of the father borders on the ludicrous. Even a short time later, technical improvement can be discerned. "Bridget O'Donnel and Children" (*ILN*, December 22, 1849) **[Figure 16]**, in their all-but naked wretchedness, form an image that is more scathingly critical of the political conditions of the time than does the "Woman Begging at Clonakilty" (*ILN*, February 13, 1847) **[see Figure 31 page 41]**, whose shawl shrouds her hunger and modesty. The ragged clothes of the O'Donnel family expose a greater expanse of their skeletal bodies, iterating the "half-clad spectres" description in the accompanying article. Mrs. O'Donnel, with her distended body and concave chest, was the antithesis of the Victorian feminine ideal, but she became in iconography a powerful metaphor for the devastated and sorrowing country.

THE MIRROR OF TRUTH

Disease claimed more Famine victims than starvation. Overcrowded workhouses, poor housing and diet, lack of clothing and heat, depression and drunkenness, "not to mention the pig in the kitchen and the middens that disgraced the frontage of every cabin in the country" (Geary 29), were factors in the spread of typhus, dysentery, smallpox and cholera. Relapsing fever was the most pernicious of all. Extreme toxemia led to internal hemorrhaging as the body disintegrated, emitting the foulest stench as it discharged and decomposed while the poor person was still alive. The vector of the Famine fevers was body lice, which multiplied rapidly in unwashed clothing and hair, and spread disease by biting into the skin of their victims, most of whom would have had immune systems already weakened by malnutrition. Lice lingered in each house for months on end and contact with the sick often proved fatal. People were terrified of contagion. The illustration of a vicar accompanying a man on his dying journey is a poignant case in point: "The Vicar sits while Mullins lies in the corner. Mullins died and 3 days later, so too did the Vicar." The poor man had buried his wife five days previously; the hut that housed the couple and their three children was less than ten feet square **[Figure 17]**, and, according to the artist, James Mahony, in order to sketch the scene, he had to stand up to his ankles in the filth upon the floor.

Figure 17 | **"Mullins's 'Hut' at Scull"** (*ILN*, February 20, 1847)

Accounts of rats gnawing at the bodies of people still alive, but too weak to fend them off, and dogs feeding at shallow graves, were never drawn. An inquest at Corbetstown, for example, recounted the death of a mother and three children drowned in a dike "saturated with mud, and frozen, having been exposed to the inclemency of the weather. The hand of one child, and part of the foot of another, devoured by rats" (*Cork Examiner,* December 4, 1846). Other reports wrote of dead babies found on their mothers' breasts, or live babies on the breasts of their dead mothers. In Schull, a dead woman was found by the roadside with a dead infant at her breast, the child having bitten off a nipple trying to squeeze a drop of nourishment from her wretched body. Such scenes offered no uplifting moral to readers; they were too awful to contemplate, let alone illustrate.

In 1847, American philanthropist Elihu Burritt found a tiny shed where the dying buried themselves:

And into this noisome sepulchre living men, women and children went down to die; to pillow upon the rotten straw, the grave clothes vacated by preceding victims and festering with their fever. Here they lay as closely to each other as if crowded side by side on the bottom of one grave. (6)

In Skibbereen, the *Cork Examiner* announced, "one third of the population will be swept away" unless the Government "be *coerced* to humanity by the indignant voice of the country" (January 6, 1847). Unmarked graves, in the form of trenches, were dug, and bodies dropped in, and covered with quicklime. The Famine represented not only the end of a way of life, but also, for many, the end of the ritual of death.

In her account of Famine illustration, Margaret Crawford notes (83, 88) the contrast between the written accounts of starvation and the "anatomical sturdiness" of many of the illustrated victims. In "A Scene in Tarmons—A Widow and Children of the O'Connell Estates on their Way to Beg Potatoes" (*PT,* February 14, 1846) **[Figure 21]**, for instance, the only one who looks underfed is the dog. Drawing starving bodies challenged not only the skills of artists, but also the conceptual frames of reference of the time, encouraging artists to filter out the worst, and allowing shorthand features, such as tattered rags, unkempt hair, dirt, and body language to function symbolically. The woman shivering by the fire in "Interior of J. Shar's Cabin" (*PT,* January 24, 1846) may look comely, but she hugs her arms to herself in a gesture used to convey her cold and hunger.

Written reports of starvation were less self-censoring. Dr. Daniel Donovan, Medical Officer to the Skibbereen Poor Law Union in West Cork, did not shirk in describing the symptoms: severe pain, insatiable thirst, an inability to get warm, "the face and limbs become frightfully emaciated; the eyes acquire a most peculiar stare; the skin exhaled a peculiar and offensive foetor, and was covered with a

Figure 21 | "A Scene in Tarmons—A Widow and Children of the O'Connell Estates on their Way to Beg Potatoes" (*PT*, February 14, 1846)

brownish filthy-looking coating, almost as indelible as varnish." When he first encountered it, Dr. Donovan initially believed the "filthy-looking coating" to be encrusted dirt, but experience taught him "that this is a secretion poured out from the exhalants on the surface of the body." His descriptions of malnutrition, causing tooth loss, swollen joints, distended stomachs and bursting blood vessels, leading to painful and distressing diseases, and ultimately death, were horrendous. He went on to explain that what "paralysed the faculties of the adult served to sharpen the instinct of the child: babies scarcely able to speak became expert beggars." But, most distressingly, he outlined:

the total insensibility of the suffered to every other feeling except that of supplying their own wants ... I have seen mothers snatch food from the hands of their starving children; known a son to engage in a fatal struggle with a father for a potato; and have seen parents look on the putrid bodies of their offspring without evincing a symptom of sorrow. (382)

Much is written about what Dr. Donovan called "[t]he triumph of pestilence and the feast of death" (*ILN*, February 13, 1847), but a painful and rarely visited aspect of the Famine story is the appalling things people must have done to each other in order to survive. Donovan was one of the few to consider psychological trauma, social collapse, and the breakdown of normal human behavior. Among other horrors, he recounted how a fourteen-year-old boy slit the throats of two children to get some Indian meal. Elsewhere, there are accounts of cannibalism from the West of Ireland, one involving a family so hungry that the mother ate the flesh of the leg of her dead son, another, in Mayo (*Times*, May 23, 1849), of a starving man who was said to have "extracted the heart and liver ... [of] a shipwrecked human body ... cast on shore" and eaten it.[9] Breandán Mac Suibhne describes a "grey zone" of morality in which people must have resorted to any and all means to survive, "the demimonde of soupers and grabbers, moneylenders and mealmongers, and those among the poor who had a full pot when neighbours starved, and the poorhouse bully who took the biscuit from the weak" (2013). No such transgressions were illustrated, the wonder is any made it to the written page.

Charles Trevelyan, assistant secretary to the Treasury and chief administrator of relief, argued: "The real evil with which we have to contend is not the physical evil of the Famine, but the moral evil of the selfish, perverse and turbulent character of the people" (qtd. in Hart 99). He believed that the Famine was "the direct stroke of an all-wise and all-merciful Providence" (201), concluding with some satisfaction: "Supreme Wisdom has educed permanent good out of transient evil." (1) So, as the Famine bit deeper, newspapers moved from the descriptive to the interpretative, blaming the Irish for their own woes. *Pictorial Times* perceived "a painful deterioration of character ... becoming darker, deeper, and more destructive in each generation that succeeds" (January 31, 1846), to the extent that by the end of the Famine a report in *The Illustrated London News* wondered whether too few had died:

Figure 22 | "A 'Street Door' in Tarmons" (*PT*, January 24, 1846)

Were it not for Ireland, Great Britain would be ... too happy to deserve a friend"...[t]he aboriginal trait remains, and even cholera and famine have been lenient enough to spare a sufficient number of murderers to perpetuate the race, and to retard the improvement and the prosperity of the country. (October 30, 1852)

Racialization of poverty had been the guiding principle of government policy on the Famine. David Lloyd argues:

[a] long standing political and ethnological objectification of the Irish as a population trapped in premodernity and incapable of attaining to subjecthood permitted the view ... that the Famine was providential, a godsend that made possible the clearing of the land of a redundant people.

He notes that the shattering of the people and their culture was:

less a question of intentions than of the structural effects of colonialism itself. The Famine, whatever else we wish to say about its contours and meaning, must be seen as a colonial catastrophe."(220–21)

The more tragic (or radical) the Irish became, the more they were dehumanized illustratively. "A 'Street Door' in Tarmons" (*PT*, January 24, 1846) **[Figure 22]**, for example, shows a barely human child. At this time, the pseudo-science of phrenology, in which man's moral and intellectual development could be read from his physiognomy, was gaining credibility. John Beddoe's "Index of Nigrescence" placed the Irish close to Cro-Magnon man and the "Africinoid" races (258). L. Perry Curtis, Jr. (1997) describes how the facial angles and structures were thought to position the various races on the evolutionary scale. The prognathous jaw and low forehead ascribed to the Irish were considered evidence of low evolutionary status **[Figure 23]**.

Figure 23 | "Irish Physiognomy" (*ILN*, October 7, 1843)

Figure 24 | "The Irish Frankenstein" *(Punch*, 1843)

Figure 25 | "Connaught Man" *(ILN*, August 12, 1843)

The satirical magazine *Punch* specialized in drawing the simian Irish **[Figure 24]**, but racial stereotyping also occurred in the illustrated newspapers, where it was perhaps all the more destructive for purporting to be realistic **[Figure 25]**.

If the *character* of individuals was seen to reside in their *appearance*, the bias of the artist and/or draftsman was inevitably going to break through. It follows, therefore, that issues of 'truth' were complicated by allegiances and nationality. Nevertheless, the pictorial newspapers informed their readers that their written and pictorial accounts were "the result of recent tours made by the artists and authors," and insisted on their accuracy (*ILN*, August 12, 1843). But the very idea of using illustration as *evidence* was problematic. It was not just *facts* that were at stake, *values, emotions*, and *ideologies* also came into play, framing both words and images in their search for truth. This can be seen in the controversy that surrounded the exposé of the conditions of Daniel O'Connell's tenants in Derrynane in Co. Kerry.

Between August 1845 and January 1846, the *Times* produced a series of articles by its "Commissioner," Thomas Campbell Foster, who took O'Connell to task for the condition of "his wretched tenantry," declaring that "amongst the most neglectful landlords who are a curse to Ireland, Daniel O'Connell ranks first" (December 25, 1845). So extreme were Foster's descriptions that they were met with widespread incredulity, encouraging other papers, pictorial papers among them, to seek to contradict or corroborate his reports. The result was a stampede of Commissioners, visual and textual, to the Iveragh Peninsula that reverberated as far as Australia (*Melbourne Argus*, June 9, 1846). Irish newspapers defended O'Connell, and the high moral ground, insisting that unfavorable reports were politically motivated. With this story, the pictorial newspapers, with their capacity to use images to confirm text, and text to concretize images, came into their own. Even the *Times* felt obliged to back up its own story, sending William Howard Russell who confirmed everything, and added:

> *the observations I am about to make are mere statements of fact, as plain as the sun in noonday. I shall not pretend to say that Mr. O'Connell is a good or a bad landlord—whether your Commissioner is right or wrong; but describing things as I found them—as they are visible to every eye—I shall leave the public to judge the points at issue, and content myself with assuring you that no person, consistingly* [sic] *with truth, can deny one iota of the statements I am about to make.* (December 19, 1845)

INTERIOR OF CLUVANE'S HUT.

Figure 26 | **"Interior of Cluvane's Hut"** *(ILN*, January 10, 1846)

In an interesting assertion of the primacy of the visual over the verbal, *The Illustrated London News* sent an artist only, but this had its limitations. In this artist's accompanying report, he described how "the great majority of the houses [are] without windows or chimneys, ill-thatched and filthy, surrounded by cesspools and semi-liquid manure" (January 10, 1846), but admitted how his experience of "half-naked children, pigs, cows, filth, and mud, was such a picture as I cannot draw." The one cabin he did draw was comparatively well appointed, while his other images tended towards the topographical **[Figure 26]**. Was this artist straddling a middle course between the pro- and anti-O'Connell factions of the press? As we don't know his identity, crucial issues of ideology cannot be explored, but one interpretation might suggest an Irish artist sensitive to the embarrassments of the poverty.

Figure 27 | **"Cabin at Ardcara"** *(PT*, January 31, 1846)

The contentions surrounding accuracy provoked *Pictorial Times* to send its own Commissioner(s) in January 1846. Although the paper does not attribute either the text or images, we know it was William Howitt, the poet and well-known literary figure. According to a number of other newspapers, Howitt appears to have acted as both artist and writer (*Leeds Times,* January 10, 1846; *Daily News*, March 23, 1846). Howitt also published a long article in *Tait's Magazine* (January 1846), perceived as "a set off to the reports of the *Times* Commissioner." But the fact that the wily O'Connell invited Howitt to stay with him in Derrynane naturally gave rise to questions of objectivity. Howitt conceded that the question of O'Connell's tenantry was "ticklish ground;" he prevaricated by providing an encomiastic account of O'Connell's lavish hospitality, but wrote little of his practices as a landlord. He enthused about the wild romantic scenery, but was not invited to visit the hovels of the poor, and mused that "it might have been considered a poor return" for Mr. O'Connell's kindness to have done so. While Howitt admitted being "occupied in a round of family entertainments," such as hare-hunting with Mr. O'Connell (*Leeds Times*, January 10, 1846), O'Connell's supporters read Howitt's articles as exoneration.

As it was with *The Illustrated London News* report, this story also exhibits image/text tensions. The *Daily News* defended Howitt's description of the hovels as "well written and true." "Cabin at Ardcara" (*PT*, January 31, 1846) **[Figure 27]**, for example, was described as so pestilential that the inhabitant "can only enter his wretched hovel on all fours, like a beast going into his den," but the accompanying illustrations suggested "a degree of comfort, and evidence of property in the shape of pigs and poultry" which belie the facts. (March 23, 1846)

Some confusion remains. Is the description of Howitt as "artist" accurate, as no other pictorial work by this writer is known? And if Howitt was indeed the artist as well as the writer, is it credible that he saw nothing of the appalling interiors of Derrynane Beg, given the detail evident in most of the sketches? Or, were there two people involved? We know that another artist, Frederick N. Sheppard, was also dispatched to Ireland by *Pictorial Times* and produced the cluster "Pictorial Facts" (including "A 'Street Door' in Tarmons," (*PT*, January 24, 1846) **[see Figure 22 page 30]**). As no other known work by Sheppard has come to light either, it would seem that *Pictorial Times* was running two pictorial Commissioners to produce what was after all a substantial number of illustrations on the subject of O'Connell as landlord.

Both *The Illustrated London News* and *Pictorial Times* illustrations fail to portray the poverty their texts describe, but the imbalance is less evident in *Pictorial Times*. Given that the latter illustrations grounded the poverty and neglect more explicitly, it is difficult to see how Howitt could not have witnessed them (although the accusation that he over-endowed the peasants with livestock and poultry is credible). The conditions of the peasantry were, one would think, *unimaginable* to a Victorian gentleman who had never previously seen them. In his written articles in *Pictorial Times* (January 24 and 31, 1846), however, Howitt, camouflaged his reluctance to criticize O'Connell by quoting from the *Times* extensively:

> *The distress of the people was horrible. There is not a pane of glass in the parish, nor a window of any kind in half the cottages. Some have got a hole in the wall for light, with a board to stop it up. In not one in a dozen is there a chair to sit upon, or anything whatever in the cottages beyond an iron pot, and a rude bedstead with some straw on it; and not always that. In many of them the smoke is coming out the doorway; for they have no chimneys ... Unaided and unguided, the poor creatures are in the lowest degree of squalid poverty.*
> (qtd. in *PT*, January 24, 1846)

On visiting the same estate in January 1846, *Pictorial Times* homed in, both textually and visually, on the cabin of one Maurice O'Connell **[Figure 28]**—more "a grave than a dwelling, so narrow, dark, damp, and fetid is it." And there "in that abode, which we have accurately depicted," the newspaper continued, "Maurice O'Connell vegetates **[Figure 29]** ... He knows nothing and does little, and though better off than many—he is still at a very low point of human existence." The *Daily News* picked up the story (March 23, 1846), reporting that "the half peasant's portrait has produced a beautiful confusion in the people's minds, as to its being or not being the eldest son of Mr. O'Connell." Not surprisingly, it described the inclusion of this illustration as an "unworthy trick" (March 23, 1846), saying that this "is not the way to put down Repeal." *Pictorial Times* responded (January 24, 1846) by insisting that their sketches were "faithful, unexaggerated representations, drawn in every case on the spot."

ARDCARA — INTERIOR OF MAURICE O'CONNELL'S CABIN.

Figure 28 | "Ardcara—Interior of Maurice O'Connell's Cabin" (*PT*, January 24, 1846)

Figure 29 | **"Maurice O'Connell of Ardcara"** (*PT*, January 24, 1846)

The following week, it reiterated the point:

Our aim from the first has been truth, nor shall anything induce us to swerve from it: ... We must yield our task to the details of the artist, and the imagination of the reader ... forming a spectacle of accumulated and indescribable abominations, at which humanity, we say not benevolence, shudders with instinctive and overwhelming repugnance. And yet, in this very condition, twenty, thirty, forty such hovels may be seen together, the abodes of a man, his wife, and two, three, four, five, six, seven, or eight children, all in darkness—all in abject ignorance—all eating, drinking, sleeping, in a bestial state ... which is absolutely pestilential. (January 31, 1846)

The response of the *Times* to these illustrations in *Pictorial Times* was remarkably thorough. In a lengthy disquisition on truth and artifice in text and image, the *Times* found its pictorial competitor wanting; it identified two common faults: content deficiency and excessive elaboration—the former caused by a lack of ability, and the latter by poor judgment:

The writer who exaggerates loses credence, is certain of contradiction, and, when the exaggeration is exposed, of having his past or future descriptions and conclusions disregarded. If, however, his description bears the test of examination, that which was before but description becomes authority, valued because of its truth. So with artists, a feeble pencil overlooks—cannot, in fact, delineate that which is before it—cannot seize on salient points. But the still more common fault of artists is to strive at picture making—no matter what the subject, still aiming at a pretty picture. (qtd. in *PT*, February 7, 1846)

As the *Times* saw it, *Pictorial Times* failed to "seize on the salient points," going on to sneer that "with feastings and civilities and assiduous attention," its artist was "completely befooled," but it acknowledged that "the misery is beginning to tell upon [him], and at length we are getting a peep at the truth" (qtd. in *PT*, February 7, 1846). Conceding that there were some "faithful drawings," the *Times* dismissed others as "unlike the reality as any imaginative artist could wish his drawings to be;" however, it deemed excellent the "Interior of Maurice O'Connell's Cabin at Ardcara" (*PT*, January 24, 1846) **[see Figure 28 page 36]**— "whether as a drawing simply, or as a truthful picture," and the "Group of Cabins at Ardcara" (*PT*, January 31, 1846) **[Figure 30]** was acknowledged as "faithful and truth-telling." Then, reverting to attack its true quarry, the *Times* pushed the pen home: "we can only say, that great must be the powers of face of the man who, with such a tenantry, can presume to lecture the landlords of Ireland, and hold himself forth as a pattern of a landlord" (February 3, 1846).

Figure 30 | "Group of Cabins at Ardcara" (*PT*, January 31, 1846)

In response, *Pictorial Times* graciously accepted the praise for those illustrations "which have established the extreme wretchedness and squalid misery of a portion of the O'Connell estate, as being no less faithful than graphic," but it took exception to the accusation of "*couleur de rose.*"

We can assure the Times, *and, if necessary, prove to the public that, in an artistical sense ... we have reflected it from the mirror of truth itself—if fidelity in art-delineation can furnish the quicksilver to such a glass. We are not open, therefore, to our contemporary's mild rebuke; and the rose colour, so far as our O'Connell illustrations are concerned ... Is it said we have sketched a solitary case? That here and there may be such a hovel, but that such cabins appear only occasionally and rarely in the 'Emerald Isle?' We at once meet the supposition, and demonstrate its fallacy.* (February 7, 1846)

The Illustrated London News called on the Irish artist James Mahony to vouch for its veracity. Mahony was both correspondent and illustrator, and his contributions can be examined as a unit, in contrast to the usual anonymous and separate artist-writer contributions. His editors cited his Irishness as proof of his objectivity (although one could equally argue the opposite). That he exhibited as a fine artist was something for *The Illustrated London News* to brag about, and so he was named whenever possible. His standing was such that he was accorded several double-page spreads in which he raised public awareness of the Famine from a British domestic problem to a major international humanitarian cause, provoking James Michael Farrell to describe Mahony's work as "an object lesson in the rhetoric of display" (66).[10]

Mahony's primary mission was to authenticate. His stories frequently describe his experiences as eyewitness, invariably in the first person: "I started from," "I saw," "I met," "I learned," "I heard," "I witnessed," even "I was heart-sick." And he corroborated his stories by traveling with the extraordinary Dr. Daniel Donovan, extracts of whose "Diary of a Dispensary Doctor" appeared in the *Southern Reporter* in 1847 and 1848, and were replicated in international newspapers. Through his contributions to medical journals—the *Lancet*, the *Dublin Journal of Medical Science* and the *Dublin Medical Press*—Donovan became the world authority on famine, the first to identify how famine cachexia led to atrophy and attenuation, causing the starving body to become autophagous—in effect, to tragically eat itself.

A MASS OF HUMAN PUTREFACTION

Newspaper illustration owes its existence to the sketch which came into its own during the Romantic period. No longer a preliminary or preparatory work *to* something, it became an aesthetic object itself, leading to an unprecedented level of experimentation in both form and content. The speed of execution generated immediacy not achievable in the more protracted techniques of fine art painting. Spontaneous, natural and, therefore, it was thought, more truthful, the sketch earned a newly acquired authority that was based on its very "unfinished-ness."

Another important and recent development was the vignette, developed by Thomas Bewick, and exploited by avant-garde artists. In the hands of some, it lent itself to the subject of death. Both Géricault's *The Raft of the Medusa* (1818–19) **[see Figure 7 page 12]** and Delacroix's *Death of Sardanapalus* (1827) (Musée du Louvre) feature a densely centered composition, with indeterminate peripheries. This imbues the images with a centrifugal force, while the open extremities imply narrative expansion beyond the boundaries (Rosen and Zerner, 1984). The non-defined boundaries encouraged the viewer to follow the narrative imaginatively, beyond what they could see literally. In the case of illustrations in newspapers, the bleeding out of the image also created a powerful dialogical connection between the image and the text.

When James Mahony got to West Cork, his home county, he despaired at representing what he saw: "I can now, with perfect confidence, say that neither pen nor pencil ever could portray the misery and horror.... and privation as I trust it may never be again my lot to look upon" (February 13, 1847). More than other correspondent, Mahony recognized how the people had become coarsened by the routinization of death: "so hardened are the men regularly employed in the removal of the dead from the workhouse, that I saw one of them, with four coffins in a car, driving to the churchyard, sitting upon one of the said coffins, and smoking with much apparent enjoyment" (*ILN*, February 20, 1847). But his Famine illustrations demonstrate a determination not to dehumanize his subjects, and he devised a number of ways to avoid doing so.

In his avoidance of melodrama, and in his insistence on the dignity of the victims, Mahony used the vignette to great effect—as a bridge between his illustrations and his text, as a way of screening off detail too horrific to draw, and as a way of employing the power of suggestion for what occurs beyond the image.

If a child is an effective symbol of vulnerability, how much more so is a dead child? In "Woman Begging at Clonakilty" (*ILN*, February 13, 1847) **[Figure 31]**, the shattered mother looks the viewer in the eye. The lower half of the spectral figure bleeds out, and she appears to emanate, evoking simultaneously an apparition of the Virgin and Child, and the Pietà. The text describes a woman "carrying in her arms the corpse of a fine child, and making the most distressing appeal to the passengers for aid to enable her to purchase a coffin and bury her dear little baby." Paradoxically, in its simplicity, the image is metonymic of the Famine, but without the text we would not even know that the baby was dead. Here text and image work together to assail the reader. The image raises the possibility that the "fine" child might be alive, the text banishes the hope. Margaret Kelleher argues that "when the maternal body ... becomes the place of death, a primordial breakdown has occurred" (23). The personification of a disintegrated Ireland as a mourning mother was designed to elicit sympathy, but it also contributed to a victim-view of Irish suffering. It is significant that Mahony does not overplay this, indeed the strength of his portfolio lies in the range of his narrative methods. Undoubtedly, he was aware of many conflicting issues: the need to convince skeptics of the existence of the Famine; the risk of alienating readers who were approaching Famine fatigue; the need to shield the delicate of disposition from the true awfulness; the shifting of blame onto the Irish; the propagation of stereotypes; and British fears of retaliation.

Figure 31 | "Woman Begging at Clonakilty" (*ILN*, February 13, 1847)

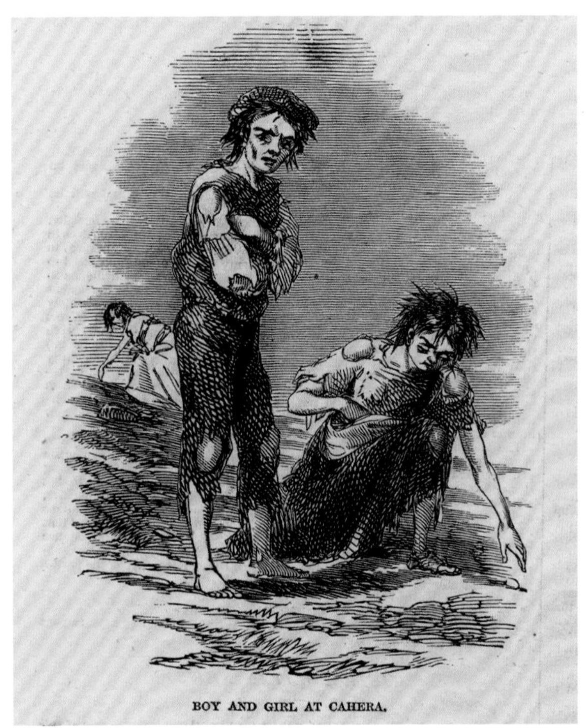

Figure 32 | "Boy and Girl at Cahera" *(ILN, February 20, 1847)*

Alongside grieving mothers, orphaned children feature in Famine imagery. "Boy and Girl at Cahera" (*ILN*, February 20, 1847) **[Figure 32]** is a stark picture of two hungry children, alone yet struggling to survive in a frightening world. We are invited to complete the bigger picture from the compressed image. By focusing on the frontal stare of the traumatized boy, the artist compels us to imagine what the *child* sees. The malnourishment of the children is evident in their thin, spiky hair, although they "appear sturdy, contrary to what one would expect in prolonged famine conditions" (Crawford 81). The power of these images, however, lies in the economy of detail and delineation. Here the scavenging children are treated as individuals, but the vignette setting suggests that they are representative of a whole class.

Like the Clonakilty mother, the boy from Cahera engages directly with the viewer and, in addition to other emotions, provokes latent anxieties in the viewer that suggest fear of contagion, underlying reproach, or reprisals to come. On the one hand, his huddled arms suggest cold, hunger and disease, and on the other, they connote defiance. His sister, scrounging for a morsel to eat—"like [a dog] after truffles"—(*ILN*, December 22, 1849) can also be subjected to different readings. Charlotte Boyce argues, "[t]hese Irish children are objects of pity, but they are also carefully 'othered,' dissociated from the civilized gentility of the intended reader" (436). There are ambivalences in even the most realistic images that allow them to be read in different ways, making them palatable to people of opposing points of view. Such illustrations then can simultaneously evoke sympathy, be read as an indictment of the government and landlords, or reinforce negative stereotypes about the Irish.

The orthodoxy is that Mahony produced the most graphic images of the Famine; in fact, he often declined to cross the threshold, protecting the privacy of the poor, turning the backs of the subjects to the viewers, occluding the effects of Famine on their ravaged bodies. This stratagem obviated visual detail (as in the actual appearance of hunger in its victims). Blocking the view of the spectator—having the starving and the dying showing their backs—paradoxically has the effect of drawing the viewer further into the visual field, positioning the viewer to see what the subjects see. The back view also suggests a stifling of feeling, not unlike the act of turning away to hide one's expressions of pain. Attuned to the dignity of the people, Mahony was determined to avoid voyeurism and objectification.

Figure 33 | **"The Hut or Watch-house in the Old Chapel Yard"** (*ILN*, February 13, 1847)

Akin to the notion of the turned back, Mahony also employed the trope of the closed door. The closed door forces the spectator to imagine the horrors behind while simultaneously protecting the dignity of the victims. At "Harrington's Hut," Mahony found four dead bodies. A fifth "fell in the doorway; there, in all probability to die; as the living cannot be prevailed to assist in the interments, for fear of taking the fever" (February 13, 1847). Faced with a scene that was not so much unrepresentable, but indecent to represent, Mahony's solution was to close the door. Similarly, "The Hut or Watch-house in the Old Chapel Yard" (*ILN*, February 13, 1847) **[Figure 33]** combined both a back view and a blocked door. For this scene, Dr. Donovan had led Mahony to an evicted family, who, perceiving themselves by virtue of contagion untouchable, struggled to the cemetery in Skibbereen and buried themselves in a small shed, seven-feet long by six wide, *surrounded by a rampart of human bones, which have accumulated to such a height that the threshold, which was originally on a level with the ground, is now two feet beneath it. In this horrible den, in the midst of a mass of human putrefaction, six individuals, males and females, labouring under most malignant fever, were huddled together, as closely as were the dead in the graves around ... I thrust my head through the hole of entrance, and had immediately to draw back, so intolerable was the effluvium.* (February 13, 1847)

THE VILLAGE OF MIENIES.

Figure 34 | "The Village of Mienies" *(ILN*, February 20, 1847)

One of the most horrific occurrences related to a man called Leahey from Dromdaleague, Co. Cork. In early 1847, Leahey died. His wife and children remained with his corpse "until the putrescent exhalations from the body drove them from their companionship with the dead." Several days later, people heard loud snarling, and on entering, found the gnawed and mangled skeleton of Leahey "contended for by hungry dogs." Whilst sketching the house, Mahony learnt that it was the man's mother who found the dogs eating her son, having gone out to beg for money for a coffin in which to bury him. Such stories defy pictorialization. Rather, the hooded child and crouching figure **[Figure 34]** indicate the melancholy nature of the scene, the cloud overhanging the house, the darkened door and the open cesspit hint at the horror within, but ultimately, it is left to our imagination. Mahony's eloquence lay in his restraint.

THE TRIUMPH OF PESTILENCE AND THE FEAST OF DEATH

In many respects, as Primo Levi articulates in *The Drowned and the Saved,*

compassion itself eludes logic. There is no proportion between the pity we feel and the extent of the pain by which pity is aroused. ... Perhaps it is necessary that it can be so. If we had to and were able to suffer the sufferings of everyone, we could not live. (56)

From the outset, the government was determined not to apply the resources of its vast empire to alleviate the suffering, even though Ireland had been part of the United Kingdom since 1800. But it was at pains to deflect criticism. According to *The Illustrated London News,* Britain's response to the Famine constituted "the most magnificent charity that was ever recorded in history, and saved her helpless and almost hopeless millions from otherwise certain death" (August 30, 1851).

But compassion did come from abroad.[11] India was the first to send money. Pope Pius IX personally donated, and in March 1847 issued an encyclical appealing for support. The Tsar of Russia, and the President of the United States also gave. Choctaw Native Americans, and even convicts on board a prison ship in London were moved to send a contribution. Several slave churches from the Caribbean, and southern states of America, a children's orphanage and prisoners in Sing Sing Prison, New York, likewise. Of course, relief also came from more expected sources in the United States, from Irish Catholics there (although inevitably, in America, relief became embroiled with demands for Irish political independence). When the Sultan of Turkey wanted to send £10,000, he was persuaded to reduce it so as not to exceed Queen Victoria's donation of £2,000. Each act of foreign generosity, therefore, was perceivable as an indictment of government inaction, and was rarely illustrated.

The second potato failure in 1846 led to the formation of the Central Relief Committee of the Society of Friends. Although the Quakers only numbered about 3,000, by the end of 1847 (when their funds ran out) they had distributed some £200,000 worth of relief, without any religious conditions (proselytism or souperism—giving food to the poor in return for their conversion to Protestantism—was a matter of bitter resentment).

The compassion of the Quakers was unparalleled. The distribution of food and seed; employment in agriculture, fisheries, and industry; and instruction in new crop techniques were among the practical projects initiated by the Quakers. Following the closure of the public works schemes, and before the poor law unions set up soup kitchens, the Quakers opened kitchens in Waterford, Enniscorthy, Limerick, Clonmel and Youghal. In the article and illustration, "Central Soup Depot, Barrack-Street, Cork" (*ILN*, March 13, 1847), the artist, James Mahony, described how 1,300 people a day were fed in this one depot.

The government's short-lived kitchens were meticulously constructed and run. The soup produced in "M. Soyer's Model Soup Kitchen" (*ILN*, April 17, 1847) **[Figure 35]** in Dublin was, according to Chef Soyer, delicious, but the comfort was cold. The bowls and spoons were chained to the tables. When the food was ready, a bell was rung and a hundred people admitted, grace was said, the bell rung again for them to begin, and "a sufficient time" allowed them to eat their quart of food. By allowing each person six minutes, one thousand could be fed per hour. And for those who wished to make the soup themselves, Soyer's *Charitable Cookery; or, the Poor Man's Regenerator* could be purchased. As soup kitchens were perceived as benevolent and non-politically contentious, there are many illustrations in the pictorial press of the day.

Figure 35 | "M. Soyer's Model Soup Kitchen" (*ILN*, April 17, 1847)

Towards the end of 1847, the British government announced that the Famine was over, although there were almost five more years to go. Five years later, the first "post-Famine" harvest **[Figure 36]** elicited a disturbingly bucolic illustration that belied the lingering physical and mental distress of people—supporting the government's denial of the persisting conditions. By 1848 donations had largely dried up, and the poor were left to the mercilessness of Irish landlords, as the government had by now pronounced that Irish property must pay for Irish poverty. But, as Emily Mark-Fitzgerald notes, "[f]ar from a simple exchange of funds from wealthy to poor, the codes of charitable intent and action are inextricably constituted in the ideological system inhabited and imposed by the donor" (195). Charity donations from Britain to Ireland could be easily derailed by inappropriate tone or imagery. The illustrated newspapers had huge influence in this regard,

Figure 36 | "Harvest in Kilkenny" (*ILN*, October 30, 1852)

and they knew it. As *The Illustrated London News* put it, "it is a part of our nature that the sufferings of some should be the occasion for the exercise of virtue in others" (December 22, 1849). One of the missions of Famine illustration therefore was to show blameless suffering in the form of women and children—the "deserving poor." To this end, one of the most emotive of all Famine images is "Miss Kennedy Distributing Clothes at Kilrush" (*ILN*, December 22, 1849) **[Figure 37]**.

When Captain Arthur Edward Kennedy took up his post as Poor Law Inspector in the Kilrush Union in 1847, he predicted that by May 1848 there would be total starvation (Senior 227). A few days before Christmas 1849, his seven-year-old daughter piled her clothes onto a pony and trap to distribute to poor children. In this image, an elderly woman, "crouching like a monkey, and drawing around her the only rag she had left to conceal her nudity" has a big tear rolling down her face.

Figure 37 | "Miss Kennedy Distributing Clothing at Kilrush" (*ILN*, December 22, 1849)

Surrounded by the sunken eyed, and hollow cheeked, the little Kennedy girl, with her father standing behind her, hands clothing to two starving children her own age. It is an awful transaction between innocents, and though the contemporary viewer might wince at the overt Victorian sentimentality, it remains among the most iconic images of the Great Hunger.

When public works—building roads that led nowhere and walls that surrounded nothing—were beyond the physical capacity of the starving, these projects were abandoned. Over one million people were in need of relief, but evictions, emigration and deaths continued to rise. Vast numbers resorted to begging. And when all else failed, it was the workhouse. Much as people resisted it, many clamored for admission. The interiors of workhouses remained largely beyond artists' reach, although there are many images of the forbidding exteriors. In the workhouse, it was ordained that "inmates should be worse clothed, worse lodged and worse fed than independent labourers in the district" (O'Connor, 61). Few who entered left alive, and if they did, they left in workhouse stripes, like escaped convicts.

Figure 38 | **"The Day after the Ejectment"** (*ILN*, December 16, 1848)

Figure 39 | "Village of Moveen" (*ILN*, December 22, 1849)

When the crop failed over successive years, and the poor were unable to pay their rents, many landlords, realizing that they could increase their income by turning their land to pasture, set about clearing it of tenants. In some instances, they did not even wait for them to default. Evictions generally required considerable force, and in this the landlords were protected by armed soldiers and constabulary and aided by hired "wreckers." In "Ejectment of Irish Tenantry" (*ILN*, December 16, 1848) [see **Figure 14** page 21], the landlord's agents drag the beseeching family out of their house. This was a relatively well-off family, but the following week, in "The Day after the Ejectment" (*ILN*, December 16, 1848) **[Figure 38]**, we see them reduced to living in a ditch, exposed to the sleet and rain. Notwithstanding the rather histrionic stance of the shattered father, the artist has not been thwarted by the chain of production in preserving the tender image of gentle solicitation of the young mother comforting her little baby.

Whole communities were evicted, houses unroofed, villages turned to pasture **[Figure 39]**. It is estimated that between 1846 and 1853, over a half a million people were made homeless. Eviction was frequently a sentence of death. The deserted villages "look like the tombs of a departed race, rather than the recent abodes of a yet living people ... forced to burrow in holes, and share, till they are discovered, the ditches and the bogs with otters and snipes." The devastation was such that one artist professed relief "at seeing one or two half-clad spectres gliding about, as an evidence that I was not in the land of the dead." He continued "[o]ne beholds only shrunken frames scarcely covered with flesh—crawling skeletons, who appear to have risen from their graves, and are ready to return frightened to that abode."

The "single enormity" of Mrs. Gerrard's "heart-sickening and revolting" evictions in March 1846 of 447 men, women and children was egregious, even by bad landlord standards. Although legal, banishing tenants "into the fields, the ditches, and the bogs," to certain death, was shocking. Even the British press acknowledged: "no crime which the law sanctions is less a crime because so sanctioned" (*ILN,* April 4, 1846). To ensure that the "wretches" could not take shelter in what remained of their tumbled cabins, Mrs. Gerrard had the foundations dug up. The "screaming of the children, and wild wailings of the mothers driven from home and shelter" were heard for miles.

Following eviction, the destitute resorted to living in "scalps," **[Figure 40]** troughs dug in the earth, two or three feet deep. The Connor family lived in a hole, roofed with sticks and turf, "laid in the shape of an inverted saucer [resembling] though not quite so large, one of the ant-hills of the African forests." But even from scalps, the poor were hunted, "like a fox, or some other vermin ... unearthed, and left even without the shelter of what may be called a preparatory grave." There were even cases of peasants being burnt out of these holes, including one of a child whose charred remains were brought out on a shovel.

Figure 40 | "Scalp of Brian Connor, near Kilrush Union-house" (*ILN*, December 22, 1849)

THE BLACK HOLE OF CALCUTTA

Irish hunger—hunger in the colonial tinderbox—was in a class of its own. Even before the Great Famine, descriptions abounded of ungovernable mobs railing against those who had food to sell but inflated prices and created scarcity. "Food Riot in Dungarvan" (*PT*, October 10, 1846) **[Figure 41]** shows an agitated mother hold her child aloft, either in entreaty or defiance. Note the loaf of bread converted to a "weapon," and beyond the reach of the people. But, as *Pictorial Times* saw it, the Irish were "what they ever were, a discontented and starving people."

Figure 41 | **"Food Riot in Dungarvan"** *(PT, October 10, 1846)*

A violent history of agrarian secret societies confirmed for many British observers the innate violence of the Irish. The reality was that, with few exceptions, most peasants were too debilitated to muster much resistance, even to eviction, and even minor protests or infractions of the law could provoke a serious response from the authorities **[Figure 42]**. On the eve of the Famine, a faction fight in Ballinhassig, Co. Cork **[Figure 43]**, broke out. When "Ranter" Sullivan gave the faction whoop, two gangs set to, but were intercepted by the police. James Mahony's illustration shows the police firing heavily into the unarmed crowd. Ten died and twenty-two were injured. The Coroner's Inquest concluded "Justifiable Homicide," confirming the official view that the slaughter of innocent civilians was a necessary part of controlling an unruly population.

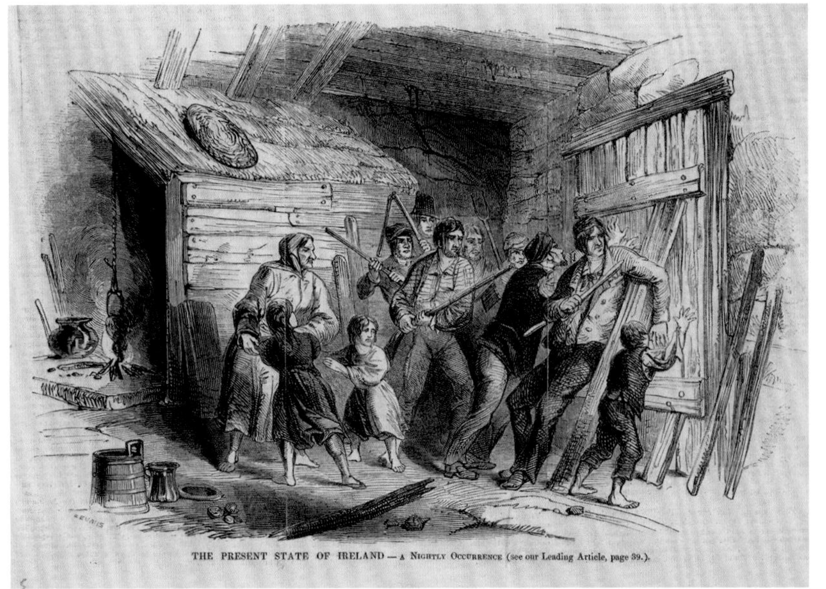

THE PRESENT STATE OF IRELAND — A NIGHTLY OCCURRENCE (see our Leading Article, page 39.).

Figure 42 | "The Present State of Ireland — A Nightly Occurrence" (*PT*, January 14, 1847)

The struggle in Ireland for Catholic Emancipation (granted in 1829) had given rise to a mass-movement. Capitalizing on this, Daniel O'Connell set up the Repeal Association to campaign for the abolition of the Act of Union of 1800. The aim was to revert to the constitutional position achieved by Henry Grattan in the 1780s, but with Catholic involvement in a new Irish parliament. In October 1843, under pressure to repress the movement, British Prime Minister Sir Robert Peel had indictments drawn up against O'Connell and eight "traversers" on charges relating to conspiracy and subversion.

[COUNTRY EDITION.

THE CONFLICT AT BALLINHASSIG.—SKETCHED BY MR. MAHONY, CORK.—(SEE NEXT PAGE.)

Figure 43 | "Conflict at Ballinhassig" (*ILN*, July 12, 1845)

O'Connell's decision to submit to the consequent state trials was seen as a betrayal of the nationalist cause by the more militant Young Irelanders. Following O'Connell's release, an *Illustrated London News* report depicted him on the balcony of his Dublin home. The illustration features a double apex, showing O'Connell, the Liberator, looking down from the first floor balcony of his home, as an exultant crowd look up, flinging their hats in the air **[Figure 44]**. The report on the triumphal tour of

O'CONNELL AT THE BALCONY, IN MERRION-SQUARE, DUBLIN.

Figure 44 | **"O'Connell at the Balcony, in Merrion-Square, Dublin"** (*ILN*, September 14, 1844)

MR. O'CONNELL, IN HIS TRIUMPHAL CAR.

Figure 45 | "Mr. O'Connell, in his Triumphal Car" (*ILN*, September 14, 1844)

O'Connell through the streets in a carriage drawn by six dappled grays, "bearing three stories... and profusely decorated with purple velvet, gold fringes [and] two large arm-chairs, covered with purple velvet and gilding," occupied by O'Connell and his son **[Figure 45]**, played upon English anxieties, which were further exaggerated by the accompanying illustration **[Figure 46]** which showed a menacing, simian-featured agitator celebrating O'Connell's release and rallying the surrounding crowd with unmistakable intent.

NIGHT-SCENE IN A DUBLIN-STREET.

Figure 46 | "Night-scene in a Dublin-street" (*ILN*, September 14, 1844)

Figure 47 | "Forging Pikes—a Recent Scene in Ireland" (*ILN*, August 5, 1848)

The illustration, "Forging Pikes. A Recent Scene in Ireland" (*ILN*, August 5, 1848) **[Figure 47]**, with its dramatic use of chiaroscuro, is full of menace, and the following week's illustration, "The Affray at the Widow McCormack's House, on Boulagh Common," (*ILN*, August 12, 1848) **[Figure 48]** has a demonic quality suggestive of a whole country out of control. Both depict the uprising of July 29, 1848, organized by the Young Ireland movement, which in reality was a shambolic and brief encounter ended quickly by armed police. Britain quickly realized that no serious rebellion was forthcoming, but made use of it to justify further coercion.

Figure 48 | "The Affray at the Widow McCormack's House, on Boulagh Common" (*ILN*, August 12, 1848)

BURIED IN THE DEEP

The failed rebellion hardened British sympathies for evicted Irish peasants. The role of landlords in forcing a mass exodus remains one of the most shocking aspects of the Famine. When people ceased to be useful "they were cast away like broken tools" (*ILN*, April 26, 1851). In May 1851, *The Illustrated London News* reported "one [ejectment] each minute so that, taking an average of souls to each family we will have 300 per hour." The total number of evictions in Connemara alone during the early months of that year was 4,000.

Figure 49 | "Irish Emigrants Leaving Home—The Priest's Blessing" (*ILN*, May 10, 1851)

In their hundreds of thousands, the homeless and hungry boarded what became known as "coffin ships" to flee Ireland. Although precise figures are unknown, over one million people emigrated during the Famine years 1845–52, and some estimates suggest that about 30 percent of those did not survive. The pain of emigration bit deep. Many would never see their loved ones again. "Irish Emigrants Leaving Home—The Priest's Blessing" (*ILN*, May 10, 1851) **[Figure 49]** shows a family on their knees, and the community turnout for the tearful farewell. A companion illustration features Jack Sullivan's family "goin to Ameriky." At the time of this illustration, so great were the numbers leaving that there was fear that there would not be enough people left to cultivate the land, even though landlords continued to evict their tenantry "with as much virulence as ever" **[Figure 50]**.

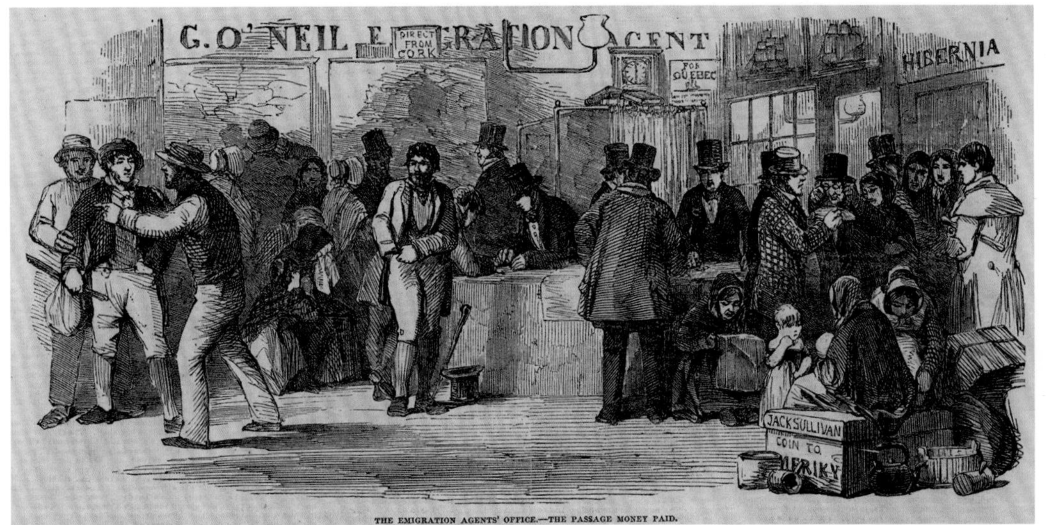

THE EMIGRATION AGENTS' OFFICE.—THE PASSAGE MONEY PAID.

Figure 50 | "The Emigrant Agent's Office— The Passage Money Paid" (*ILN*, May 10, 1851)

The Illustrated London News wrote myopically of the "splendid emigrant ships," transporting on average 250,000 people per annum. As with previous Famine illustrations, there was a discrepancy between the images and the texts in describing the reality of the emigrant experience. "Steam Communication between Galway and New York: Departure of the Viceroy Steamer from the Dock Quay, Galway" (*ILN*, June 8, 1850) **[Figure 51]** shows a rather jaunty group of emigrants being waved off enthusiastically from the shore. And "Dancing between Decks" (*ILN*, July 6, 1850) **[Figure 52]** conveys a jolly picture of a leisurely cruise to America. But "Emigration Vessel, Between Decks" (*ILN*, May 10, 1851) **[Figure 53]** shows the tight dormitory conditions, and "Tide of Emigration to the United States and the Colonies," and "Searching for Stowaways" (*ILN*, July 6, 1850) **[Figure 54]**, are darker images that hint at the terrible experiences of the transatlantic refugees; however, no image matches the horror of the written eyewitness accounts.

DEPARTURE OF THE "VICEROY" STEAMER FROM THE DOCK QUAY, GALWAY.

Figure 51 | "Departure of the 'Viceroy' Steamer from the Dock Quay, Galway" (*ILN*, June 8, 1850)

Figure 52 | "Dancing between Decks" (*ILN*, July 6, 1850)

Although the majority survived emigration, it was a dreadful experience. Shipping regulations were lax; many of the vessels were minimally converted cargo ships, owned by rapacious profiteers; "brokers" sold tickets at inflated prices; emigrants were given inadequate food and dirty and insufficient supplies of water. Tenants of Lord Palmerston (Foreign Secretary in Lord John Russell's Government) were so destitute that they were reported traveling almost naked. Twenty percent of his tenants died on the Canadian route in 1847 alone, and about half of Major Mahon's Strokestown tenants died in transit. Captain Denham, in his *Report to the Board of Trade* (May 21, 1849) described *Virginius* passengers sitting upright and in conditions so cramped that motion was impossible for the entire journey: "The common offices of nature, including vomiting from sea-sickness, were consequently done on the spot

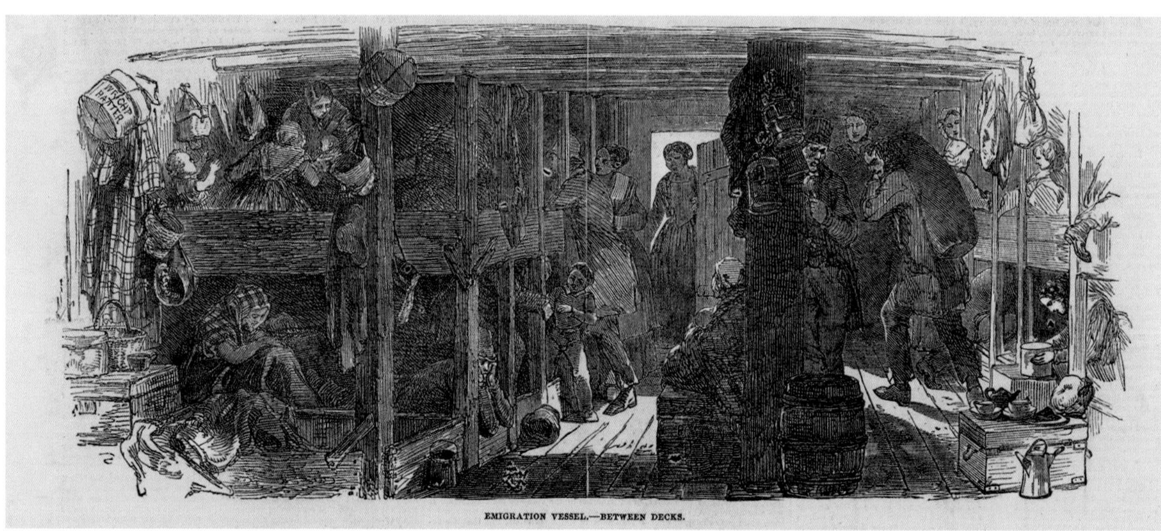

Figure 53 | "Emigration Vessel—Between Decks" (*ILN*, May 10, 1851)

Figure 54 | "Searching for Stowaways" *(ILN*, July 6, 1850)

... The passengers and cattle were indiscriminately mixed together; the sea and urine pouring on their clothes from the animals, and they stood in the midst of filth and mire" (qtd. in Neal 77–78). On September 17, 1847, the lead editorial in the *Times* elaborated on the emigrants' experience:

... consigned to encampments of the dying and of the dead, spreading death wherever they roam, and having no other prospect before them than a long continuance of these horrors ... The worst horrors of the slave trade which it is the boast of the ambition of this empire to suppress at any cost have been reenacted in the flight of British subjects from their native shore ... The Black Hole of Calcutta was a mercy compared to the holds of these vessels.

Stephen de Vere, son of an Irish landlord from Co. Limerick, made the three-month steerage passage to Quebec, in 1847:

Before the emigrant has been a week at sea he is an altered man. How can it be otherwise? Hundreds of poor people, men, women and children of all ages, from the drivelling idiot of ninety to the babe just born, huddled together without light, without air, wallowing in filth and breathing a fetid atmosphere, sick in body, dispirited in heart, the fever patients lying between the sound, in sleeping places so narrow as almost to deny them the power of indulging, by a change of position, the natural restlessness of the disease; by their ravings disturbing those around, and predisposing them, through the effects of the imagination, to imbibe the contagion; living without food or medicine, except as administered by the hand of casual charity, dying without the voice of spiritual consolation, and buried in the deep without the rites of the Church. (qtd. in Woodham-Smith 226)

Those below deck voyaged in the dark. To add to the terror, dreadful scenes of drunkenness took place as the crew sold alcohol to starving and dehydrated passengers. And arrival brought its own horrors. When the authorities realized how disease-ridden were the immigrants, they set up quarantine stations that held the sick, until they died, or were fit to travel on.

So they died in Ireland, they died at sea, they died while the ships lay at anchor, and they died in quarantine. At Grosse Île, Quebec, in May 1847, there were forty vessels stretched two miles down the St Lawrence River filled with sick and dying immigrants waiting to come ashore. The sheds and tents of the quarantine station were already full to overflowing, and thousands more were still to come.

In the shadow of catastrophe, people who had never ventured beyond their own townlands found themselves transported to another continent, from a rural to an urban landscape, to an alien English-speaking world where people feared them for their diseases and despised them for their Irishness and their Catholicism. Those who remained behind struggled to come to terms with their personal losses in a devastated country, and not least, with the guilt of the survivor.

Figure 55 | Lilian Lucy Davidson, *Gorta*

Between 1845 and 1852, one million excess people died of hunger and disease, and over one million emigrated (two-thirds of these to the US alone). By the early years of the twentieth century, over five million Irish had traveled to North America.[12] Over a fifty-year period from 1845, the population of the country was halved. This was how Ireland was modernized.

It was almost a hundred years before the Great Hunger became the subject of art again in the harrowing painting exhibited in 1946 by Lilian Lucy Davidson called *Gorta* **[Figure 55]**. Previously known as *Burying the Child*, and now part of Ireland's Great Hunger Museum, here we glimpse the legacy of the Famine as a traumatized family look past one another, into nothingness.

ENDNOTES

[1] The once sparse historiography of the Famine, dominated by the work of Cecil Woodham-Smith, is now substantial, and has been broadened to include new cross-disciplinary research and interpretation. Major contributors include Christine Kinealy, Cormac Ó Gráda, Peter Gray, James S. Donnelly, Gearóid O'Tuathaigh, Breandán Mac Suibhne, David Nally, Luke Gibbons, David Lloyd, L.P. Curtis, Joe Lee, Kerby Miller, Terry Eagleton, Oona Frawley, Marguérite Corporaal, Enda Delaney, Kevin Whelan, Ciarán Ó Murchadha, John Kelly, Laurence M. Geary, Chris Morash, Margaret Kelleher, Catherine Marshall, Emily Mark-Fitzgerald, John Crowley, Melissa Fegan, Joel Mokyr, William J. Smyth and Mike Murphy.

[2] For a discussion on Irish artists' responses to the Famine, see Catherine Marshall, "Painting Irish History: the Famine," *History Ireland*, no. 3 (Autumn 1996), 47–49.

[3] See John T. Koch, ed. *Celtic Culture: A Historical Encyclopedia*. Santa Barbara, CA: ABC-Clio, Vol 1, 2006.

[4] The first study of the pictorial press was undertaken by Mason Jackson in 1885; it was over a hundred years later before the topic was revisited by Brian Maidment, Peter W. Sinema, Niamh O'Sullivan, Emily Mark-Fitzgerald, Gerry Beegan, Joshua Brown, Leslie Williams, James Michael Farrell and Patrick Leary.

[5] For discussion on the paintings of Ireland's Great Hunger Museum, see Niamh O'Sullivan, "Lines of Sorrow: Representing Ireland's Great Hunger" in *A Guide to Ireland's Great Hunger Museum*, 2012.

[6] When the block was reassembled, it was delivered to the electrotyper who prepared the pages for the printers.

[7] For more on illustration during the Land War period, see Niamh O'Sullivan, *Aloysius O'Kelly: Art, Nation, Empire*. Dublin: Field Day, 2010.

[8] Within the fine art tradition, the panorama suggested aesthetic disinterest. Mahony drew on this in his funeral images to distance viewers from the reality.

[9] Cormac Ó Gráda is one of the few to address the topic of cannibalism during the Famine. See, "Eating People is Wrong: Famine's Darkest Secret?"(2013). <http://www.ucd.ie/t4cms/WP13_02.pdf>. Web. 8 August 2014.

[10] Vincent van Gogh purchased Mahony sketches, including the famous "Boy and Girl at Cahera"(*ILN*, February 20, 1847) from *Sketches in the West of Ireland* (4 on 1 sheet), Vincent van Gogh Museum, Amsterdam.

[11] For further discussion, see Christine Kinealy, *Charity and the Great Hunger in Ireland: The Kindness of Strangers*, 2013.

[12] For more on the demographics of the Famine, see Smyth, William, J. "'Mapping the People': The Growth and Distribution of the Population," *Atlas of the Great Irish Famine*. Cork: Cork University Press, 2012.

WORKS CITED

Angelou, Maya. *I Know Why the Caged Bird Sings.* 1969. New York: Random House. 1969. Print.

Beaumont, Gustave de. *Ireland: Social, Political and Religious.* 1839. Eds. T. Garvin and A. Hess. Cambridge, MA: Belknap Press of Harvard University Press, 2006. Print.

Beddoe, John. *The Races of Britain: A Contribution to the Anthropology of Western Europe*. 1862. Bristol and London: 1885. Print.

Boyce, Charlotte. "Representing the 'Hungry Forties' in Image and Verse: The Politics of Hunger in Early-Victorian Illustrated Periodicals." *Victorian Literature and Culture* 40. 2 (2012): 421–49. Print.

Burritt, Elihu. *A Journal of a Visit of Three Days to Skibbereen, and its Neighbourhood.* London: Charles Gilpin, 1847. Print.

Clarendon Papers. Irish Letter-Books. Bodleian Library. Oxford. Print.

Crawford, Margaret. "The Great Irish Famine 1845–9: Image Versus Reality." *Ireland: Art into History*. Eds. Raymond Gillespie and Brian P. Kennedy. Dublin: Townhouse Press, 1994. 75–88. Print.

Crowley, John, William J. Smyth, and Mike Murphy, eds. *Atlas of the Great Irish Famine*. Cork: Cork University Press, 2012. Print.

Curtis, Jr., Lewis Perry. *Apes and Angels: The Irishman in Victorian Caricature*. 1971. Washington: Smithsonian Institution Press, 1997. Print.

Donovan, Daniel. "Observations on the Peculiar diseases to which the famine of the last year gave origin and on the morbid effects of insufficient nourishment." *The Medical Examiner: A Monthly Record of Medical Science* Vol. 4, June 1848. Print.

Farrell, James Michael. "'This Horrible Spectacle': Visual and Verbal Sketches of the Famine in Skibbereen." *Rhetorics of Display*. Ed. Lawrence J. Prelli. Columbia, SC: University of South Carolina Press, 2006, 66–89. Print.

Franklin, Benjamin. *The Life of Benjamin Franklin, Written by Himself.* 3 vols. Ed. John Bigelow. Cambridge: Cambridge University Press, 2011, Vol. 2. Print.

Galt, John. *The Life, Studies and Works of Benjamin West, Esq., President of the Royal Academy of London* Part II. London: T. Cadell and W. Davies, 1820. Print.

Geary, Laurence. "Epidemic Diseases of the Great Famine." *History Ireland* 4.1 (Spring 1996): 27–32. Print.

Gibbons, Luke. *Limits of the Visible: Representing the Great Hunger*. Hamden, CT: Ireland's Great Hunger Museum/Quinnipiac University Press, 2014.

Hart, Jenifer. "Sir Charles Trevelyan at the Treasury." *English Historical Review* LXXV. 294 (1960): 92–110. Print.

Hughes, Robert. *Goya*. London: Harvill Press, 2003. Print.

Jackson, Mason. *The Pictorial Press: Its Origins and Progress*. London: Hurst & Blackett, 1885. Print.

Kelleher, Margaret. *The Feminization of Famine: Expressions of the Inexpressible*? Cork: Cork University Press, 1997. Print.

Kinealy, Christine. *Charity and the Great Hunger in Ireland: The Kindness of Strangers.* London: Bloomsbury, 2013. Print.

Kozloff, Max. *Renderings: Critical Essays on a Century of Modern Art.* New York: Simon and Schuster, 1968. Print.

Levi, Primo. *The Drowned and the Saved.* 1988. London: Abacus, 2013. Print.

Lloyd, David. "The Indigent Sublime: Specters of Irish Hunger." *Representations* 92 (Fall 2005): 152–85. Print.

Mac Suibhne, Breandán. "A Jig in the Poorhouse." *Dublin Review of Books*, 32 (April 8, 2013). <http://www.drb.ie/essays/a-jig-in-the-poorhouse> Web. 8 August 2014.

Maidment, Brian. "Representing the Victorians—Illustration and *The ILN*." <http://gale.cengage.co.uk/images/BrianMaidment1.pdf>. Web. 1 May 2014.

Mark-Fitzgerald, Emily. "Towards a Famine Art History: Invention, Reception, and Repetition from the Nineteenth Century to the Twentieth." *Ireland's Great Hunger: Relief, Representation, and Remembrance.* Ed. David A. Valone. Lanham, MD: University Press of America, 2009: 181–201. Print.

Marshall, Catherine. "Painting Irish History: the Famine." *History Ireland* 4.3 (Autumn 1996): 47–49. Print.

Mitchell, W. J. T. *Iconology: Image, Text, Ideology.* Chicago: University of Chicago Press, 1986. Print.

Mitchel, John. *The Last Conquest of Ireland (Perhaps)*. 1862. Ed. and introd. Patrick Maume. Dublin: UCD Press, 2005. Print

Neal, Frank. *Black '47: Britain and the Famine Irish*. London: Palgrave Macmillan, 1997. Print.

O'Connor, John. *The Workhouses of Ireland: The Fate of Ireland's Poor*. Dublin: Anvil, 1995. Print.

O'Sullivan, Niamh. *Aloysius O'Kelly: Art, Nation, Empire*. Dublin: Field Day, 2010. Print.

––––"Lines of Sorrow: Representing Ireland's Great Hunger." *Ireland's Great Hunger Museum Inaugural Catalogue*, Hamden, CT: Quinnipiac University, 2012. Print.

Rosen, Charles and Henri Zerner. "The Romantic Vignette and Thomas Bewick." *Romanticism and Realism: The Mythology of Nineteenth-Century Art*. New York: Viking Press, 1984. Print.

Senior, Nassau William. *Journals, Conversations and Essays Relating to Ireland.* Vol. 1, London: Longman, 1868. Print.

Smyth, William, J. "'Mapping the People': The Growth and Distribution of the Population." *Atlas of the Great Irish Famine*. Eds. J. Crowley, W. J. Smyth, and M. Murphy. Cork: Cork University Press, 2012. Print.

Sontag, Susan. *Regarding the Pain of Others*. New York: Picador, 2003. Print.

Trevelyan, Charles E. "The Irish Crisis." London: Longman, Brown, Green and Longmans, 1848 [reprinted from *Edinburgh Review* CLXXV (January 1848)]. Print.

Woodham-Smith, Cecil. *The Great Hunger: Ireland 1845–49*. London: Hamish Hamilton, 1962. Print.

Weld, Isaac. *Statistical Survey of the County of Roscommon*. Dublin: Royal Dublin Society, 1832. Print.

IMAGES

Figure 28

"**Ardcara — Interior of Maurice O'Connell's Cabin**"
Pictorial Times
January 24, 1846

Figure 29

"**Maurice O'Connell of Ardcara**"
Pictorial Times
January 24, 1846

Figure 30

"**Group of Cabins at Ardcara**"
Pictorial Times
January 31, 1846

Figure 31

James Mahony

"**Woman Begging at Clonakilty**"
The Illustrated London News
February 13, 1847

Figure 32

James Mahony

"**Boy and Girl at Cahera**"
The Illustrated London News
February 20, 1847

Figure 33

James Mahony

"**The Hut or Watch-house in the Old Chapel Yard**"
The Illustrated London News
February 13, 1847

Figure 34

James Mahony

"**The Village of Mienies**"
The Illustrated London News
February 20, 1847

Figure 35

"**M. Soyer's Model Soup Kitchen**"
The Illustrated London News
April 17, 1847

Figure 36

"**Harvest in Kilkenny**"
The Illustrated London News
October 30, 1852

Figure 37

"**Miss Kennedy Distributing Clothing at Kilrush**"
The Illustrated London News
December 22, 1849

Figure 38

Fitzpatrick

"**The Day after the Ejectment**"
The Illustrated London News
December 16, 1848

Figure 40

"**Scalp of Brian Connor, near Kilrush Union-House**"
The Illustrated London News
December 22, 1849

Figure 41

"**Food Riot in Dungarvon**"
Pictorial Times
October 10, 1846

Figure 42

"**The Present State of Ireland — A Nightly Occurrence**"
Pictorial Times
January 14, 1847

Figure 43

"**Conflict at Ballinhassig**"
The Illustrated London News
July 12, 1845

Figure 44

"**O'Connell at the Balcony, in Merrion-Square, Dublin**"
The Illustrated London News
September 14, 1844

Figure 45

"**Mr. O'Connell, in his Triumphal Car**"
The Illustrated London News
September 14, 1844

Figure 46

"**Night-scene in a Dublin-Street**"
The Illustrated London News
September 14, 1844

Figure 47

"**Forging Pikes — a Recent Scene in Ireland**"
The Illustrated London News
August 5, 1848

Figure 48

"**The Affray at the Widow McCormack's House, on Boulagh Common**"
The Illustrated London News
August 12, 1848

Figure 49

"**Irish Emigrants Leaving Home — The Priest's Blessing**"
The Illustrated London News
May 10, 1851

Figure 50

"**The Emigrant Agent's Office — The Passage Money Paid**"
The Illustrated London News
May 10, 1851

Figure 51

"**Departure of the 'Viceroy' Steamer from the Dock Quay, Galway**"
The Illustrated London News
June 8, 1850

Figure 52

"**Dancing between Decks**"
The Illustrated London News
July 6, 1850

Figure 53

"**Emigration Vessel — Between Decks**"
The Illustrated London News
May 10, 1851

Figure 54

"**Searching for Stowaways**"
The Illustrated London News
July 6, 1850

Figure 55

Lilian Lucy Davidson
1879–1954

Gorta
1946
Oil on canvas
27.5 x 35.5 in

Images provided by Ireland's Great Hunger Museum, Quinnipiac University, unless noted otherwise.

ABOUT THE AUTHOR

Niamh O'Sullivan is Professor Emeritus of Visual Culture (National College of Art and Design). She writes on nineteenth-century Irish and Irish-American art and popular culture. She won the Irish-American Cultural Institute 'Award for Pioneering Irish-American Scholarship' in 1998 and 2003. Her book, *Aloysius O'Kelly: Art, Nation, Empire* was published by Field Day in 2010. She curated the millennium exhibition *Re:Orientations. Aloysius O'Kelly: Painting, Politics and Popular Culture* at the Hugh Lane Municipal Gallery of Modern Art, 1999–2000. She is a director of the Irish Museums Trust, on the advisory board of the International Network of Irish Famine Studies and a member of the advisory committee of the Royal Irish Academy *Art and Architecture of Ireland Volume V: Twentieth Century*. She is Curator of Ireland's Great Hunger Museum.

ACKNOWLEDGMENTS

My appreciation and thanks to Ciarán Deane, Grace Brady, Christine Kinealy, Luke Gibbons and Michael Foley for helpful comments; to Claire Tynan for picture research; to Ciarán Deane for editing; to Mary Glynn for assistance with Ireland's Great Hunger Museum Database; and to Brad Collins and Jessica Cassettari of Group C Inc, for design and production.

IRELAND'S GREAT HUNGER MUSEUM DATABASE

The Tombs of a Departed Race is the first essay to use the Ireland's Great Hunger Museum Database of extensive pictorial news documents of the Famine (1845–52). Launched in 2014, this Database is housed at Quinnipiac University. Access is via the museum website www.ighm.org. The expectation is that scholars of many disciplines will benefit greatly from this resource, and further research will be generated.

SERIES EDITORS

Niamh O'Sullivan
Grace Brady

IMAGE RESEARCH

Claire Tynan

DESIGN / PRODUCTION MANAGEMENT

Group C Inc, New Haven
Brad Collins
Jessica Cassettari

ACKNOWLEDGMENT

Office of Public Affairs, Quinnipiac University

PUBLISHER

Quinnipiac University Press

PRINTING

GHP Media

ISBN 978-0-9904686-3-9

Ireland's Great Hunger Museum
Quinnipiac University

3011 Whitney Avenue
Hamden, CT 06518-1908
203-582-6500

www.ighm.org